BRITAIN IN OLD PI

COLERAINE

& THE CAUSEWAY COAST

VIVIENNE POLLOCK
& TREVOR PARKHILL

SUTTON PUBLISHING LIMITED

Sutton Publishing Limited
Phoenix Mill · Thrupp · Stroud
Gloucestershire · GL5 2BU

First published 2000

Reprinted in 2001, 2002

Copyright © The Trustees of the National
Museums & Galleries of Northern Ireland, 2000

British Library Cataloguing in Publication Data
A catalogue record for this book is available from
the British Library.

ISBN 0-7509-2229-X

Typeset in 10.5/13.5 Photina.
Typesetting and origination by
Sutton Publishing Limited.
Printed in Great Britain by
J.H. Haynes & Co. Ltd, Sparkford.

The Giant's Stacks at Port Moon, part of the world-famous complex of volcanic geological features known as the Giant's Causeway.

CONTENTS

Introduction   5

1. Castles & Early Settlement   9

2. Churches & Christian Monuments   19

3. Crossing the Gap   29

4. On the Move   39

5. Harbours & Shipping   47

6. The Sea's Harvest   61

7. A Living from the Land   69

8. Townscape & Street Scenes   81

9. Stop A-While   105

10. Wish You Were Here   117

Acknowledgements   128

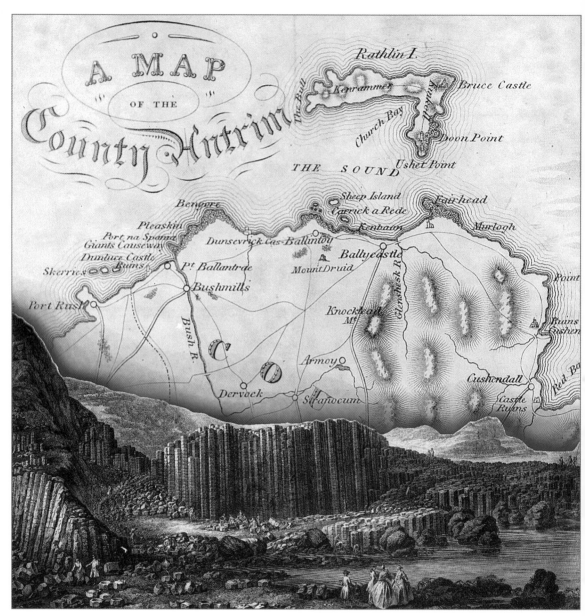

This very fine François Vivares engraving of the Giant's Causeway was made from one of a pair of famous paintings executed by Mrs Susannah Drury in 1740 and circulated across Europe; here, it has been superimposed on a contemporary map of the Causeway Coast, showing settlements between Coleraine and Ballycastle.

INTRODUCTION

The town of Coleraine, situated 5 miles from where the long-travelled waters of the River Bann finally reach the sea, takes its name from the Irish *cul rathain* meaning 'ferny corner', a fittingly romantic description for a place of such antiquity and beauty. The area is ringed with archaeological treasures of great importance, the most historic of which is the 9,000-year-old Mesolithic site on the southern outskirts of the present town, now recognised as the earliest known human settlement in Ireland. 'Ferny corner' also traditionally refers to the patch of ground, reputedly the site of the Church of St Patrick, in the town centre, presented to St Patrick when he was welcomed to the locality during his fourth-century mission to Ireland; further strong and significant links between the Coleraine area and the early Christian missions of St Columba, St Comgall and St Fiachra establish the region as a key destination in the early Christian diaspora.

The story of Coleraine and the Causeway Coast embodies the argument that the history of Ireland and its people is a product of the mingling – not always peacefully or purposefully – of cultures from far beyond its shores. Successive waves of settlement and visitations in the last 1,500 years, involving Celts, Vikings, Normans, English, Highland and Lowland Scots, have been influenced by the strategic significance of its position. Indeed, the historical and geographical importance of the coastline between Coleraine and Ballycastle are tellingly illustrated by the fate of those Spanish Armada ships which, blown off course while fleeing from their defeat by Sir Francis Drake in the English Channel in 1588, foundered on the spectacular and stormy North Antrim coast. Artefacts retrieved some thirty years ago from the wreck of the galleas *Girona*, which sank off the Giant's Causeway, remain some of the most popular items on display in the Ulster Museum.

The arrival of the Normans in Ulster from the end of the twelfth century led to the construction of a bridge across the Bann and a castle at Killowen and provided the nucleus of a settlement at Coleraine. It also meant that the region thereafter became something of a focal point for the battles waged by the armies of Edward Bruce against the Normans at the beginning of the fourteenth century.

In the early seventeenth century the Plantation of Ulster – it was the last of the four provinces of Ireland to be planted by the Crown – was centred on a number of planned towns, of which Coleraine was one of the finest examples. More than that, it was central to the settlement of the new county of Londonderry – formerly named the county of Coleraine – by a group of twelve London livery companies who

Dunluce Castle and the Giant's Causeway electric tram, with the broad sweep of Portrush's East Strand curving into the distance behind.

established a holding company, the Irish Society. Defensive walls were built with three gates, remembered only in the street names Kingsgate and Bridgegate, and in the street now called Long Commons, where townsmen could graze cattle outside the ramparts. Virtually all other signs of the Plantation town are now sadly vanished – the last house from this period was excavated in New Row in the 1980s. None the less the broader than usual streets radiating from the Diamond – as the central square in these planned settlements is known – are today a lasting testimony to its importance as a Plantation town nearly four centuries ago.

Coleraine was incorporated by royal charter in 1613 and from then began to assume its role as a town and port serving the counties of Antrim and Londonderry. Its strategic position led to it being besieged during the revolt of 1641 and its embroilment in the later struggle in Ireland between Jacobite and Williamite armies (1689–91). The charter had recognised Coleriane's pre-eminence as a seaport, and its economic activity had, during more peaceful times in the seventeenth century, enabled it to become by the 1680s the third largest town in Ulster, behind Derry and Armagh in size, but far ahead of Belfast.

In the eighteenth century ships from the ports of Coleraine and Portrush added their passengers to the significant stream of emigrants who found their way from Ulster to colonial North America. Coleraine's gradual prosperity as a market town and port for the region mirrored the development throughout Ulster of linen manufacture in the eighteenth century, to the extent that the name 'Coleraines' was given to a specific type of linen goods. Inland trading access to the town and the port was greatly facilitated from the late 1730s by the turnpike road from Antrim. Towards the end of the century it was second only to Dublin in the production of whiskey, much of which was exported, along with locally produced timber and salmon. The latter was especially abundant in the Bann: in the late eighteenth century the famous traveller Arthur Young saw as many as 1,452 salmon scooped up in one net at one time.

By 1841 Coleraine was the sixth-largest town in Ulster, with a population of 6,255 souls, and its solid mid-century prosperity was embodied in the construction in 1859 of its grand Town Hall. The workhouse (which later became the hospital) opened in 1841, one of over 130 established throughout Ireland in the years 1839 to 1842. Its presence helped cushion the town and its outlying communities from the worst excesses of the Great Famine. The first signs of potato blight were recorded in the Coleraine workhouse minutes in early October 1845: one of the first reports anywhere in Ireland of what would become a massive social disaster.

The arrival of the railway in the 1850s helped the town to benefit from the linen boom of the 1860s, when cotton supplies dried up and linen was king. With the construction in 1860 of the first railway bridge across the Bann, Coleraine became a main line station for the Northern Counties line, serving Portrush, Portstewart and towns all along the coast to Londonderry, while the Derry Central line linked the town with its hinterland as far as Cookstown.

It was by then increasingly clear that the town's progress was based on the extent to which it served the needs of the surrounding countryside. This was demonstrated by its interdependence with nearby Portrush from the mid-nineteenth century. The construction of a harbour at Portrush (1827–38) created an outport for Coleraine, which thereafter developed its trading role substantially. By the 1830s, 160 ships were trading from the port, taking out oats, bacon and butter, and bringing in coal, tea, sugar and iron. Both Portrush and Portstewart were among the leading seaside resorts which, from the later decades of the nineteenth century, would provide holiday and day-tripper attractions on an increasing scale.

Many of these holiday-makers came from Scotland – a tradition which lasted until very recent times – and one of the underlying themes portrayed in this book is the close relationship over the centuries between the Causeway Coast, including Rathlin Island, and Scotland. The views of Dunluce Castle, occupied by the MacDonnells until the dramatic collapse of its kitchens over the sheer cliff during a tempestuous storm in 1639, represent both Scottish links and the historical romance which the sometimes savage scenery of this region has been known to inspire.

In the later decades of the nineteenth century the new manufacture of garments, turbines and agricultural implements added to Coleraine's relative prosperity. This capacity to adapt to economic trends was again evident in the post-war period, when the acrylic manufacturing industry, firstly in the form of the American firm Chemstrand, then Monsanto, was established in the late 1950s.

Beach football at Portrush, 1950s style.

One of the town's long-standing characteristics has been its good name for educational provision. This has included national and endowed schools, including the Honourable the Irish Society School, a model school, a technical college, Coleraine Academical Institution and Coleraine High School. The arrival in 1968 of the New University of Ulster, Northern Ireland's second university, acknowledged that tradition. It also developed the town's role as a regional centre, with the Coleraine campus from 1984 one of four belonging to Northern Ireland's University of Ulster.

The Causeway Coast has, sadly, not remained untouched by the last thirty years of civil and political unrest. But the devastation left by the huge terrorist bomb in Coleraine in 1992 has largely been made good, and the town has reclaimed its pleasantly bustling character as the 'trim little borough'. And the equally destructive explosion in Ballycastle in 1970 has given rise to a revitalised harbour area with the rebuilding of the town's Marine Hotel. The Causeway Coast has, in the midst of those modernising features which befit an increasingly popular tourist destination, retained much of the character and beauty for which it is justly famous. No one looking over the sea from Portstewart at the sun sinking below a glowing horizon could doubt that this mesmerising view inspired the song-writer Jimmy Kennedy to write the enduring classic 'Red Sails in the Sunset'. And who can think of Ballycastle without remembering Mary Anne and the dulse and yellow man immortalised in the famous ballad 'The Oul' Lammas Fair'.

CHAPTER ONE

CASTLES &
EARLY SETTLEMENT

Lough na Cranagh, Fair Head, c. 1900. Artificial islands called crannogs were used as safe dwellings particularly during medieval times. This one was built with a sophisticated dry-stone revetment.

Standing stone, Ballyvennaght, Ballycastle, *c.* 1900. Despite their ubiquity, standing stones are an enigmatic feature of the Irish landscape. A variety of functions and dates have been ascribed to these silent sentinels of the past, which may have had territorial, religious or perhaps pathfinding significances.

Only two uprights remain to support the capstone of this Neolithic passage tomb at Clegnagh near Ballintoy, the remainder having been quarried away over the centuries. Early graves such as this, and the evidence of past lives that they contain, are an important source of information about our most distant ancestors.

Standing stone, Rathlin, February 1906. This standing stone is made of chalk, an unusual choice of material for a monument of such intended permanence. In the early nineteenth century a Viking burial containing a silver brooch was uncovered at its base.

This imposing megalithic passage tomb at Mount Druid in Magheraboy townland near Ballintoy was originally ringed by two stone circles. It is also known as the 'Druid Stone', in reference to the notion that these massive graves were used as places of worship in pre-Christian times.

These two portal tombs in Ballyvennaght townland are known as the 'Cloughananca'. They form part of a much wider burial complex exposed by peat digging near Loughaveema (the 'Vanishing Lake') in the nineteenth century.

Souterrains are artificial caves built in the early medieval period, around a thousand years ago, as places of refuge. The title of this photograph – 'The Wee Folks' Cave' – reflects the belief that these often elaborately constructed stone chambers were fairy places, and that the fairies themselves would be offended if spoken about directly.

The photographer R.J. Welch at the Grey Man's Path at Fair Head. This spectacularly steep and narrow natural fissure in the cliff offers the only access to the shore below, and was primarily used by local people collecting seaweed. It takes its name, as tradition goes, either from a colony of aged hermits who lived in the large caves at the base of Fair Head; or from a holy man who came each day for prayer and meditation; or from a ghost who brought bad luck to those who saw him. The site is also associated with An Fir Lea, the storm god of the Danaan people, as in Cassan-firlea, its alternative title, and Stack-an-var-lea, a tall sea cliff on Rathlin Island opposite.

Mountsandel 'Fort', Coleraine, *c.* 1960. The date and purpose of this huge earthen-ditched mound are quite unknown – suggestions range from a large Iron Age barrow to a seventeenth-century artillery fort. Perhaps it was both! It is close to an excavated Mesolithic campsite of great archaeological importance, having produced the earliest human settlement yet found in Ireland.

Kitchen middens, Whitepark Bay, *c.* 1910. Kitchen middens are prehistoric rubbish dumps. They contain mostly animal and fish remains, but sometimes include pottery and stone tools. They are very often the only early physical evidence of human settlements.

Dunseverick Castle, *c.* 1900. The scanty remains shown here are from the gatehouse of a larger structure, which was probably refortified by Sir James McDonnell in the mid-sixteenth century. The site was possibly that of the early capital of the ancient kingdom of Dál Riada and reputedly marks the end of the Slighe Miodluachra, one of the five great roads radiating from Tara in County Meath, seat of the Irish High Kings.

Kenbane Castle was built in 1547 by Colla Dubh MacDonnell, Chief of the MacDonnells and Lord of the Glens, who occupied it (apart from a brief period after 1551) until his death in 1558. According to local tradition, in 1580 the castle was granted in lieu of pay to a Scottish captain of troops called McAllister whose descendants dwelt there until the mid-eighteenth century when the property passed by marriage to the Boyds of Ballycastle.

The setting for the famous tale of Robert the Bruce and the spider, Bruce's Castle on Rathlin Island is not strictly a castle but a high promontory defended by a wall on the landward side. The remains of ancient hearths survive within the fortification.

Dunluce Castle from the west, May 1929. Surely one of the most impressive of Irish castles, the ruins at Dunluce ('strong fortress') cover an area of almost an acre, sitting on 100ft high cliffs, washed on three sides by the sea and separated from the mainland by a 20ft wide chasm.

Dunluce Castle. The first mention of Dunluce Castle occurs in the early twelfth century, when it was attacked by Magnus Barefoot, King of Norway; in the early sixteenth century it became a stronghold of the MacQuillans until they were ousted by the MacDonnells who occupied it until it was abandoned in 1660. The tower shown here was built in the thirteenth or fourteenth century.

Inside Dunluce Castle. The pillars suggest this was a passageway converted into a room. Dunluce did not offer a comfortable living. Its perils were exposed one stormy night in 1639, during the occupancy of the Duchess of Buckingham, wife of the 2nd Earl of Antrim, when the gale-battered kitchens, together with the cook and eight servants, crashed into the sea. The duchess, who had never much liked the castle, refused to stay within its walls another night, and built instead a large courtyard house on the mainland.

Photographed before 1917, when it was acquired by the Dominican order of nuns for use as a girls' boarding school, Portstewart Castle was built in 1834 by Henry O'Hara, one of Portstewart's two landlords, possibly as a gesture of one-upmanship towards his rival. The high surrounding wall was commissioned to provide work at the time of the Great Famine.

Rock Castle, 1905. Apparently built by Henry O'Hara as a dower house for his widowed mother, Rock Castle was leased to James and Frances White of Whitehall, County Antrim, as a summer house in 1835. On 6 July that year, the house saw the arrival of their second son George, who later became famous as Field Marshal Sir George White VC, responsible for the relief of Ladysmith in February 1900 during the Boer War.

CHAPTER TWO

CHURCHES &
CHRISTIAN MONUMENTS

The elaborately carved recessed doorway and gabled hood of the entrance to St Patrick's Church, Coleraine, were erected as part of major renovations in 1883. They provide a magnificent example of the Romanesque revival style of church architecture in vogue at that time.

This remnant of a high cross at the ancient ford of Camus, near Coleraine, is a lonely survivor of a local monastery associated with St Comgall of Bangor, County Down, one of the most important ecclesiastic centres in the early Christian firmament.

This image of a much-weathered cross on the outskirts of Ballycastle shows very clearly how such remains became part of the everyday material world of contemporary people. Here, the Christian monument appears to be acting as a part of a stile.

Few examples of 'holed' crosses exist in Ireland. This one, at Bonamargy Abbey in Ballycastle, is one of two found in the area and reputedly marks the resting place of Julia McQuillan, the 'Black Nun of Bonamargy', who came to live in the gatelodge of the abbey after the dissolution of the monasteries by Henry VIII, and was buried at her own request at the entrance to the chapel so that those entering the church had to walk over her grave. Renowned for her extraordinary piety and penitence, Julia was also well known for her gift of foreknowledge, and made many famous predictions during her years at Bonamargy. The original Christian purpose of the central aperture of her cross has been lost over the centuries. Popular belief holds, perhaps inappropriately in this case, that these stones had semi-mystical properties relating to fertility and marriage.

In contrast, this old cross, on the high slopes of Glenshesk, maintains an air of mystery in its wild isolation.

The old church of St Cuthbert's near Dunluce was reportedly founded in 1306 by Scottish planters from Galloway. It fell into disrepair thereafter, but was refurbished in about 1641 and served the area until it was superseded by the church of St John the Baptist in Bushmills in 1821. In its graveyard lie the bodies of 260 men and officers who drowned when the Spanish Armada galleas *Girona* was wrecked at Dunluce in 1588.

Culfeightrin Old Church, Churchfield, near Ballycastle, is associated with the sixth-century St Fiachra. This east gable, with its fine fifteenth-century perpendicular window, is now all that remains of a substantial building measuring 100ft by 24ft on the outside, with massive walls over 3½ft thick.

The Franciscan Tertiary Friary at Bonamargy was founded at the end of the fifteenth century by Rory McQuillan. It came into McDonnell ownership after the Battle of Orra in 1559, and was burned down by them in an attack on English troops quartered there in 1584. It was repaired and remained in use until the mid-seventeenth century. The building to the left was the gate- or guest-house of the abbey, where Julia McQuillan is said to have lived, and was originally two-storeyed.

The tomb of John McNaghten, founder of the McNaghten family, who died in 1630 and was buried in the south wall of the church at Bonamargy Abbey. Others interred in the church include four Earls of Antrim, including Sorley Boye McDonnell himself (d. 1590); Francis Stewart, Bishop of Down (d. 1749); and Julia McQuillan, the 'Black Nun of Bonamargy', whose holed-cross monument is pictured on page 21.

St Thomas's, Rathlin, photographed on a Naturalists Field Club visit to the island in 1926. Previously a monastery, St Thomas's became Rathlin's only church when the monks were moved to England. It had two graveyards, the one visible at the front for Catholic interments, and one at the rear for Protestants.

The new Agherton parish church in Portstewart was built in 1905 by James Kennedy of Coleraine to the design of architect Vincent Craig. Seen here shortly after it was consecrated, the church was moved from its original out-of-town site near Agherton Old Graveyard to this more central and convenient location close to the Diamond. The area of rough ground to the right of the church is now a car park.

Built in 1845 and officially opened by the fiery preacher-politician Dr Henry Cooke, the Dunluce Presbyterian congregation was one of the first in Ulster to sanction a Gothic design for their church, albeit confined to the vestibule across the front with its pillars and decorative buttressing.

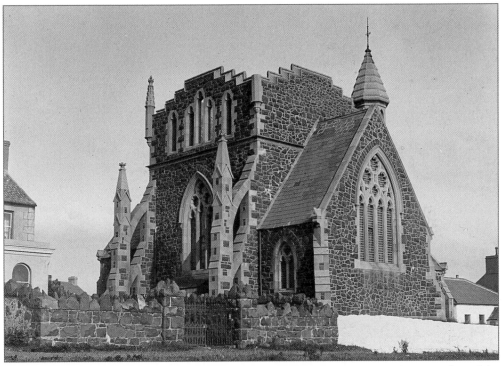

Portstewart Methodist Church in its original glory. Designed by W.J. Barre, 'the evangelist of the decorated Gothic style', and completed in 1861, his original creation, pictured here in the 1890s, included flying buttresses, a crow-stepped tower, pinnacles and, just visible, a Scots Baronial tower with a conical roof corbelled out in one corner.

Bushmills Presbyterian Church was built in 1821 on the site of the ancient church at Billy, one of the two parishes encompassing the village. Originally the congregation met near the castle at Dunluce parish, but as the town grew the ruling elder applied for permission to move 'for their convenience' to a more central meeting-spot. This was granted in 1702, but part of the congregation refused to leave Dunluce, and the situation was not resolved until 1755, when the Presbyterian Church sanctioned the ordination of a minister for Dunluce Parish as well as a minister for Billy.

Portrush Episcopalian Church, like the church shown opposite, is built of blocks of black basalt, probably from the local basalt works at Craigahulliar, with contrasting edgings. Local legend has it that labourers working on the church building to the left carved on the exterior walls the symbols of the four suits in a deck of cards after being rebuked for playing the Devil's game on holy ground.

An evocative early-morning picture of the Church of Ireland Boyd Memorial Church in Ballycastle. It was built in 1756 of stone quarried in the parish, and the entire cost of construction was met by Hugh Boyd, the local landlord. Don't be puzzled by the time told by the church clock: other views of Ballycastle suggest that when this picture was taken it had been 3.25 for a very long time!

There has probably been a church on the site of St Patrick's in Coleraine since the mid-fifth century. The present building dates in effect from 1613/14, when the communion vessels were consecrated. The view above was taken after Thomas Drew's major refurbishment of 1883 replaced the tower, extended the nave and added a north aisle. A Coleraine craftsman, Charles Magowan, was responsible for all the exterior carving.

This tiny consecrated building in Portballintrae is reputedly the world's smallest thatched church. Despite its minuscule size it serves a comprehensive range of holy functions.

CHAPTER THREE

CROSSING THE GAP

Bridges were a vital component of the network of communications within the rugged, watery landscape of the Causeway Coast region. One of the most spectacular local bridges is the swinging rope bridge at Carrick-a-rede, shown here being slung across the 90ft chasm between the seaward rock and the land, in readiness for the start of the spring salmon fishery.

Balanced like a tight-rope walker, a man with a very good head for heights poses above the towering cliffs of the Antrim Coast in this giddying view of Carrick-a-rede. Imagine crossing this flimsy, swaying bridge with a heavy basket of fish on your back, as fishermen did daily!

This narrow stone causeway leading to the gatehouse of Dunluce Castle spans a similar chasm to that at Carrick-a-rede, but in a more permanent and less dramatic fashion.

The natural symmetry of the basalt blocks of the North Star dyke as it juts into the sea at Ballycastle suggests that this was originally a man-made structure. In fact it is a geological feature, formed sixty million years ago when a flow of lava penetrated a vertical fault in the existing sandstone and then hardened.

This view of Ballycastle looks over the Margy Bridge to the quay behind. The bridge was completed in 1857 after the difficulty of establishing a sure foundation on the 'running sand' of the river bed was overcome by laying down huge sacks of sheep's wool and building on them. It still stands.

This photograph of the wooden footbridge further down river at the Margy mouth illustrates another solution to the problem of Ballycastle's beach erosion, namely the construction of sand breaks at intervals in the shallows, marked by the lines of wooden piles breaking the surface of the water in the centre and foreground.

As it expanded Coleraine began to straddle both sides of the River Bann, which enters the sea
4 miles up river. Its elegant main bridge, shown here from the Waterside (west) side of the town,
was built by Gordon Maxwell in 1844 at a cost of £145,000. The three shallow stone arches
enable it comfortably to span the 96 yards to the foot of Bridge Street on the opposite bank.

The view from the lovely four-arch basalt upper bridge in Bushmills was an artists' paradise, with
the watermills which gave the town its name sending white plumes of race water streaming into
the peaty waters of the River Bush below.

This view of Ballycastle shows the four-arch Tow railway viaduct in the foreground, leading to the railway station across the river on the right. The bridge was built by the Ballycastle Railway Company in 1880 to link Ballycastle with Ballymena via Dervock, Stranocum and Armoy, a distance of 16 miles.

The laying of the new signalling system at Coleraine railway system, in 1938. This replaced the old semaphore system of communication and allowed the gates of the level crossing to be opened and closed from the signal cabin in the background. The gates served Portrush- and Londonderry-bound trains crossing the junction of the Bushmills and Ballycastle roads. At the risk of a clipped ear, small boys could 'sail' on the gates as they swung open.

The Glenshesk viaduct carries the road from Ballycastle through Armoy to its junction with the Ballymena/Ballymoney line. It was built during the 1830s under the auspices of the new Irish Board of Public Works, which also supported the road between Ballycastle and Coleraine. The Antrim coast road, with its magnificent Lanyon-designed viaduct at Glendun, was another major local scheme sponsored by the new Board.

The metal bridge at Portrush harbour's old dock was built to carry the railway line for coal wagons to the coal quays at the extreme right of the picture. A concrete footbridge now spans its original stone piers.

This view of Bushfoot, Portballintrae, shows the apparently newly built wooden footbridge across the River Bush and, in the foreground, the stone piers of an earlier structure. The beginning of a path from the houses to the crossing is quite visible. The raised areas in the field on the left mark the old 8th green of the Bushfoot golf course.

Members of the Royal Engineers carry out the demolition in 1978 of the Victoria Jubilee bridge, built in 1887 by the Glasgow ironworkers, P. & W. MacLellan, to carry the Giant's Causeway tram across the River Bush at Portballintrae. Ironically, plans are now afoot for REME to build the bridge up again in a scheme to rerun the trams between the original depot in Bushmills and the Causeway.

The eleven-span bascule bridge at Coleraine was built by the Northern Counties Committee in 1924 to a design by their redoubtable railway engineer, Bowman Malcolm. It cost almost £100,000, and was the first Strauss underhung counterweight bridge in the British Isles. The counterweight and bascule each weighed 250 tons, and so precise was the balance that, if necessary, the bridge could be lifted by hand-cranking to afford a navigation channel 70ft wide.

This tiny whitewashed cottage at the foot of Fair Head in Ballycastle is popularly known as Marconi's Cottage. From here, it is reported, Marchese Gugielmo Marconi conducted in 1898 the trials which led to the transmission to Rathlin Island of the world's first wireless radio messages across water, a feat of communication which paved the way for the worldwide broadcasting we know today.

Fergus Greaves, from Holywood in County Down, waves to the camera before descending the cliffs of Rathlin Island on a bird-watching holiday in June 1901.

CHAPTER FOUR

ON THE MOVE

This 'racing' biplane, with its radial engine, attracted a curious crowd when it landed on Portstewart strand in 1937. Although by then planes like this were being superseded by single-wing aircraft, their supreme manoeuvrability at low speeds ensured they were kept in use for tasks such as crop spraying or, more likely on this occasion, air displays and aerial photography.

Hugh McGaghie's donkey cart outside a thatched house at Bushmills. Donkeys only became common in Ireland during the eighteenth century. By the mid-nineteenth century they had replaced working horses and ponies on many small farms, especially in more remote areas. The cart which Hugh's donkey is pulling is a small version of the standard farm cart, with removable side panels.

The smart turn-out of Marshall Brothers carriers with a load of monogrammed trunks, photographed in the early 1920s outside St Patrick's Church in Coleraine. Note the solid rubber tyres, full windscreen and oil lamps on the Fermanagh-registered lorry, and its chain drive visible behind the back wheel.

A Thorneycroft charabanc at Portstewart. By 1930 Henry's Coast Tours company was providing a half-hourly summer service along the coast road between Portrush and Portstewart for a fare of 2*d* single or 3*d* return, carrying an average of one thousand passengers per day. Charabancs were also available for day tours to Glenariff and other places of interest, and for private hire.

A mixture of pedal, horse and steam power is evident in this photograph of a steamroller that had broken down on a Glens back road in 1933. The wooden carriage behind served as accommodation for the drivers and operators who accompanied these giants as they toured from job to job.

The magnificent 'Stockbroker's Tudor' railway station at Portrush was designed by the famous railway architect Berkeley Deane Wise and built by McLaughlin and Harvey of Belfast. It opened in the spring of 1893 to replace the original station (built in 1855), which by then was proving woefully inadequate for the resort's expanding summer traffic.

Laying the cable at Coleraine railway station for the new colour signalling system which became operative in 1939. The system worked like traffic lights and included a telephone link from the signals to the signal cabin, and, just as importantly, the provision of an electric fire for the signalman's comfort.

This steam train heading to Portrush was photographed in 1968, three years after the foundation of the Railway Preservation Society of Ireland. Their earliest and most long-standing 'preservation' run was the trip from Belfast to Portrush, soon christened the 'Portrush Flyer'. The run was modelled on the pre-war Businessmen's Express service, which made the trip in 73 minutes going up and 80 minutes going down. Ticket prices were equally impressive, with an afternoon tourist excursion ticket costing just 2 shillings.

NCC Leyland PLSC2 bus at Portstewart railway station. This 31-seater railway bus, pictured here sometime after 1932, was bought by the Belfast Omnibus Company in 1927 but later sold to the Northern Counties Committee to replace the subsidised service between Portstewart and Cromore Halt which they had commissioned from Henry's Motor Service for six years following the suspension of the tramway service in 1926.

Although one of John Cromie's aims was to establish Portstewart as a seaside resort, he refused to allow the railway into the town in case it altered its quiet character. Instead he provided Ireland's first roadside steam tramway service to take passengers from the town to the railway halt at Cromore, 1½ miles away. The mock-Tudor tram terminus opened in 1899 and was designed by Berkeley D. Wise, who had also been the architect for Portrush railway station.

The steam engine proudly displayed here was acquired in 1900, soon after the tram service was established. However, a verse printed by the local paper in 1923, towards the end of the service's life, painted a less complimentary picture:

O the tram, the tram, the Portstewart tram,
Heavy and sluggish, slow as a pram.

The world's first hydro-electric tramway opened in 1883 to carry passengers between Portrush and the Giant's Causeway, a distance of 10 miles. The large building on the right is Portrush Town Hall, designed by the celebrated Belfast firm of Charles Lanyon & W.H. Lynn. Despite its summer popularity, the tramway was not profitable and closed in 1949.

The terminus near the Causeway Hotel, whose owner, William A. Traill, had been the tramway engineer. Before an overhead trolley system was introduced in 1889, the trams collected power from a raised conduction rail, seen here in the foreground. These two photographs show the early stages of the tramway's development when steam was necessary to power the tram for the last stages of its journey to Portrush. Note that the two end 'toast-rack' carriages are the same, but the one shown in the top photograph has been closed in for the passengers' greater comfort.

An apparently driverless County Down-registered 'big' Austin parked across the tracks of the Giant's Causeway tram service. The sign for the Bayview Hotel in Portballintrae, with its promise of 'parking for cars', indicates the increasing notice given by the hospitality trade to the emerging owner-driver visitor market. Perhaps it has been taken a bit too literally in this instance!

This view of Portstewart in 1929 highlights the growing attraction of the north-west as a centre for motorcycling.

CHAPTER FIVE

HARBOURS & SHIPPING

A good illustration of the hazards of navigating the tidal Bann as crowds gather on Coleraine's main bridge to watch, and no doubt offer colourful advice to, the unfortunate crew of this tug as they try to untangle their vessel.

Coleraine harbour, *c.* 1899, with the paddle tug *Confidence*, owned by local man Hugh McKeag, in the foreground and the small steam tug *Eagle* lying alongside the ship at the bridge. These two tugs were based at Coleraine and used to tow sailing vessels up and down the tricky 5-mile stretch of water between the town and the sea. *Eagle* was also used for private charter and pleasure cruising but was sold in June 1900, when it became apparent that steam coasters, which could make their way up river unaided, were replacing sailing ships.

A down river view of the bridge and the harbour beyond, taken perhaps a year later than the one above. The black top of the funnel of a steamship is visible between the masts showing over the parapet in the centre of the image.

Coleraine harbour, *c.* 1955. The boat being loaded in the foreground of this busy view is the *Bannpride*, one of a line of 'Bann' steamers operated by S.W. Coe to carry coal and other cargo between Liverpool and Coleraine. By the late 1950s steam itself was being ousted by motor-power, and scenes like this became increasingly rare.

Dockers at Coleraine Harbour, 1958. The man with the papers is Harry Murphy, newsagent, and standing from his left are Jock Adams, Jim Fleming, Bobbie Warke, Charlie Booth, Joe Fleming, Danny Vaulls, Robert Johnstone, Alex Blair and George Gage.

This sweeping view of Church Bay was taken in June 1926 and shows the small village known as The Station and Rathlin harbour, the hub of all comings and goings between the island and the mainland. The village takes its name from the complex of white houses facing the sea which were built in 1821, along with the pier and boathouse, as a coastguard station to accommodate one officer and six men. The isolated building at the junction of the main road and the shore lane to the left of the photograph was the 'Rocket House' where flares and other life-saving apparatus were stored.

This view of a tranquil sea at Ballycastle harbour gives no indication of the heavy swells to which it was prone and to which the 1930s extension of concrete and stone shown here probably contributed. The two swimmers in the centre are hanging on to Jack Coyle's boat *King George*, built by Kelly's of Portrush in 1937 and used to run mail to and from Rathlin Island.

The earliest harbour at Portstewart was built in 1832 by the local landlord John Cromie and extended in 1899 by the Board of Works at a cost of £4,000. This photograph was taken after further reconstruction work in 1910 added a new slipway and dock and shows something of the variety of craft and functions which this still tiny shelterage served.

The old fishery harbour at Portballintrae is typical of the many small ports dotted along the North Antrim coast, almost in defiance of its exposed Atlantic position. The dedication of a watch house, however, marked the port as a site of long-standing strategic importance to the coastguard. This early view shows the coastguard's boathouse, just left of centre, before it was turned for the first time into a dwelling house.

Hugh McCalmont McGildowney, seen here standing in front of the horse, built his long, metal pier in Ballycastle in 1891 to service his two steamers *Glenshesk* and *Glentow*, which traded from the port with coal and limestone, and to provide docking facilities for large ships, such as Scottish tourist vessels and cross-channel passenger steamers. McGildowney's shipping business did not survive his death, and his pier was replaced by a harbour extension in the 1930s and eventually demolished for scrap during the Second World War.

This picture of sacks being unloaded on the inner pier of Portrush harbour gives some idea of the muscle-power required in the transportation of goods in and out of the smaller harbours of the Causeway Coast. Note the metal tracks for coal wagons in the foreground, and the patience of the good horse, who must have been well used to his work.

A busy but somewhat baffling scene at the landward end of McGildowney's pier in Ballycastle as crowds of well-dressed onlookers gather to watch local fishermen 'redding out' their nets. What could they be looking at?

Fuel was scarce on Rathlin, the island having little peat, and boat-loads of turf had to be brought in to ensure supplies. Here Joseph McCurdy (standing in the boat) and John Black, behind him, transfer their cargo of peat blocks to Michael Jack Anderson in the cart, who is being helped by one of Mr Gage's serving boys.

An unusual view of Portstewart harbour against the black headland of Carrick-na-guile. The big winch in the foreground, used to haul boats up the new slipway, was an essential piece of equipment when water space was so tight. Note the sign to the right offering boats for hire.

A young girl poses somewhat awkwardly beside a massive anchor, while two boys look on from the ruins of the fishermen's cottage on the east shore of Portballintrae harbour. The white building prominently sited in the background was the coastguard 'houses'.

The bare rocks of the boat harbour at Port-na-boe ('Cow port') on the Giant's Causeway with thirteen Norwegian-style, double-ended, clinker-built, open yawls (called locally 'drondheims') brought to land. Before the cliff-top path was built by the National Trust in 1938, tourists wishing to see the full wonder of the Giant's Causeway had to hire one of these small boats, giving local fishermen a lucrative summer supplement to their earnings.

Even natural harbours sometimes needed a helping hand, as indicated by this relatively recent photograph of fishermen carrying concrete piles to shore up the boat shelter at Port-na-boe.

This picturesque view of the tiny jetty at Portbraddon at the west end of Whitepark, with its cluster of low whitewashed buildings nestling under towering cliffs, gives some idea why coastal dwellers historically regarded the sea as the great highway. Essentially, it was the easiest way out, in and around.

Two further examples of the locally favoured drondheim fishing boat shelter in the calm waters of Dunseverick harbour. Bengore Head, seen in the background, provides a perfect example of the typical profile of the basaltic headlands of the Causeway Coast, with its top half composed of perpendicular cliff and bottom half of a 45° scree.

The neat harbour at Ballintoy was remodelled in the mid-nineteenth century the better to service its two local functions as a fishing centre and an outport for stone setts. It was also an ideal spot for a day out, as this photograph of what passed as traffic congestion in the mid-1960s demonstrates.

The breathtaking panorama of the North Antrim coast is well described in this earlier view of Ballintoy harbour. The photographer would have had his back to the prospect shown above. The large outcrop of rock in the centre is Dunshammer ('fort of the shamrocks'), an Iron Age fort with an artificially flattened top.

Speedy and shallow of draft, the 1,200-ton twin screw steamer *Hazel* was built in 1907 for the Laird Line specifically to serve a daily daylight crossing from Ardrossan to Portrush, calling at Ballycastle if need be, where passengers were ferried in and out by rowing boat. In 1909 the return fare for this enormously popular crossing was 12s 6d, but sailings came to an end with the outbreak of the First World War, and *Hazel* made her last voyage to Ardrossan on 6 August 1914 with 235 people on board.

This appealing snapshot of a group of 'visitors' on Rathlin Island shows the new jetty after it was decked in 1926.

This postcard view of the 'Glasgow boat' entering Portrush shows the Laird Line steamer *Olive* crowded with visitors from the Clyde region. During the last two full seasons of this trade (1913 and 1914) over 25,000 people took advantage of this service.

A First World War sea mine, washed ashore at Portrush on 20 January 1915. A cryptic note on the back of this postcard, which bears no stamp or postmark, said simply 'No news here. Bad times.'

The foundation stone for Rathlin's first lighthouse was laid in 1849 by Mrs Robert Gage, after the purchase by the Commissioners of Irish Lights of a piece of ground at the north-east corner of the island. This view of the lighthouse and offices shows the original warning system, which consisted of two stationary lights, 295ft and 215ft above sea-level. Three cannon were kept for use during fog; these were replaced in 1920 by an electrical system which fired two shots every five minutes.

The light at Rue Point on Rathlin is a legacy of the First World War defensive strategy against U-boats, and was installed in 1915 to divert shipping southwards from the barrier of anti-submarine nets which stretched from the Mull of Kintyre to Fair Head. The outcrop of rock in the centre left, Sloak-na-calliagh, was the site of a dreadful atrocity in 1575 when Presbyterian Scots Covenanters, fighting for the Campbells of Auckenbreck, defeated the sorely outnumbered Rathlin McDonnells and put the island to the sword, hurling a great number of women and children to their deaths in the gully below.

CHAPTER SIX

THE SEA'S HARVEST

For centuries the sea and river fisheries of the Causeway Coast have been famous for their richness. Here a crew of fishermen from Portbraddon ('port of the salmon') hold up a magnificent specimen of the fish for which their home port was named.

An unusual 'artistic' image of the salmon fishery at Portrush, showing a fishing crew preparing for a voyage. Note the differences between the boat being fitted out here, and the double-ended yawls favoured by fishermen on more exposed parts of the coast.

Salmon are migratory fish, and make long journeys every year to spawn in the rivers and streams of their birth. The pattern of their journeys was well known to fishermen, who set their nets in the traditional paths of the fish as they returned each spring. This view shows salmon nets drying at Ballycastle, and gives some idea of the size and construction of such devices.

This dizzying view shows a salmon boat being lowered at Carrick-a-rede ('rock in the path'). Here the returning salmon are diverted away from the coast to swim round the island rock and into fishermen's nets, making the Carrick-a-rede fishery one of the most effective of all Irish sea-based salmon fisheries.

The Salmon Cutts on the 'fruitful fishy Bann' were originally dug in the early seventeenth century to make the river navigable for the conveyance of timber to the town, but are historically home to one of the most important Irish river-mouth salmon fisheries. Here the salmon swimming upstream to spawn are channelled into fixed nets to be retrieved later by fishermen in small boats like the one in the foreground.

Look carefully at this photograph of the Kenbane salmon fishery and you will see a line of floats extending in a curve from the land to the man in the boat. These keep the nets positioned vertically in the water to form a curtain of mesh across the path of the salmon as they travel close to shore. The mesh size was governed by law so only fish of mature size were trapped.

Salmon drift nets hanging out to dry at the tiny fishery at Portaleen Bay. The isolation of the smaller fishing communities of the Causeway Coast is well illustrated in this magnificent photograph.

Fishing boats at Portmoon (top) and Portballintrae. Salmon was not the only fish hunted along the Causeway Coast as these two photographs indicate. The wicker line basket in the boat in the foreground of the Portmoon view held the baited long lines used for the deep sea capture of cod, plaice and a variety of other flat and round fish; the round wicker 'buckie' pots seen in both images were used to trap dog whelks for bait, while the long, netted pot in the picture of Portballintrae was used for crabs and lobsters.

These fishermen are working lobster pots from the small jetty opposite the Northern Counties hotel in Portrush. The flat slabs of basalt rock behind them are famous fossil-hunting grounds.

A long-line fisherman sits in a sea-cut cave on Rathlin Island, baiting his lines with a mixture of coarse fish, starfish and whelks, his boat drawn up on the ledge beside him. This cave was evidently well found, for it had a well giving fresh water at its rear. It was put out of use by the building of the lighthouse jetty.

(*Opposite*) The rivers of the Causeway Coast were well known for the richness of sport fishing they offered. Salmon were an obvious quarry, but trout and coarse fish were also hunted. This view of anglers and onlookers on the west bank of the Bann at Coleraine shows the town's boathouse, a handsome, half-timbered and brick structure designed by the local architect W.J. Given, and built in 1900 for the Bann Rowing Club.

A gaff-rigged local trawler, its trawl warps clearly visible, working close to the quay in Portrush harbour in a scene that was carefully set up between the two-man crew of the boat and the photographer, W.A. Green. In the background to the immediate left of the boat's sail can be seen the elaborate windows of the ballroom of the Northern Counties Hotel, another local example of the work of the redoubtable Berkeley D. Wise.

Motor fishing vessels at anchor at Portrush. The introduction of engine power in the inshore fisheries was a gradual affair, and sail was not completely replaced until after the late 1920s, when more powerful small diesel engines became available. This view of the harbour shows the end of Kerr Street at the extreme right of the scene.

CHAPTER SEVEN

A LIVING FROM
THE LAND

Wild game formed an essential part of the diet of rural families. Here Rathlin's Margaret McKinley, with her shotgun, rabbit trap and ferret, demonstrates that women as well as men could be skilled hunters. Note the curved lintel of the stable door, made from salvaged ship's timber.

Hard won, carefully husbanded and neatly walled, Rathlin's arable land produced beans (for sale), barley, oats, turnips and mangels. The high stone wall at the bottom of the photograph protected the Manor House's orchard, while the large building to the left of centre was the Glebe Barn, where harvests were stored. The white dot close to the gateposts on the right is the chalk standing stone depicted on page 11.

As well as being spread directly on to fields as fertiliser, seaweed was burnt to make chemical-rich kelp, an important source of cash income for coastal communities. Both cut and drift weed were collected, dried in the sun and fired in a kiln; the glutinous mass of ash thus produced was then allowed to cool and harden, after which it was broken into lumps and shipped to Glasgow for further processing. This photograph of kelp gathering at Ballycastle shows that both men and women were involved in this manufacture, and many rents were paid on the back of it.

A typical Glens farm with its cluster of buildings, photographed in the early twentieth century against the rocky slopes of lower Knocklayde. Note the wheel-less slipe leaning against the wall beside the group of men in the foreground. This has been fashioned from a forked tree branch and was used to transport bulky loads in hilly areas where wheeled vehicles could not pass.

At first glance this farm kitchen, with its bare stone floor and meagre furnishings, speaks of a comfortless existence. Look through the door to the right, however, for a glimpse into the parlour, with its fine, mahogany display cupboard, and a different picture begins to emerge.

These young women, daughters of the McAllister farmstead in Glenshesk, are tending potatoes planted in 'lazy beds', as this system of ridges and furrows is known. This labour intensive method of cultivation was highly efficient in hilly, rocky, steep or wet ground, and traces of ancient beds can be seen in high places all around the Causeway Coast, especially when highlighted by a dusting of snow or the slanting rays of an evening sun.

A boy breaking whins against a slab to use as supplementary feed for cattle. Whin was also a popular food for horses, not only as a means of making other fodder go further, but also as a conditioner, with a particular reputation for producing a glossy coat. Note the lazy beds in the background.

Winning the hay outside Ballycastle. This photograph shows the dried hay gathered into little standing piles and, in the foreground, the piles being shaken out and stacked into haycocks. Before the days of silage, this hot, itchy, laborious work was the only way of ensuring livestock had sufficient food throughout the winter.

Michael McBride, of Torr, passing turf to a young helper in the final stages of saving sufficient fuel for the year ahead. An estimated 11 tons of turf was needed to supply an average household with heat for a year, and all the family were expected to help bring it in at the end of the summer.

Sheep were dipped after shearing to prevent the spread of parasites through the flock. Usually this was done by making them swim through a stone trough filled with disinfectant. The wooden trough being used at Black's farm at Ballylucan was a new departure, the idea, apparently, of a 'returned yankee'.

A woman spinning woollen yarn on an improved or 'small' treadle wheel outside her house in Bushmills, watched by a group of children. The contrast in finish between the finely turned wooden wheel and the rough, three-legged, low-backed chair on which she sits is notable.

Flax gatherers at the Giant's Causeway.
Flax was very labour-intensive to harvest
as it was pulled rather than cut, in order
to save as much as possible of the
internal fibres from which linen was
made. It had the reputation of being a
dirty (i.e. weedy) as well as a greedy crop,
and for these reasons many farmers were
reluctant to grow it. But it was surely
one of the most beautiful, as anyone
lucky to have seen the shimmering blue
sheen of a field in full flower will testify.

Flax dam, Ballycastle. After pulling, the flax was steeped in a pond or dam, with the sheaves or
'beets' weighted down with stones. This rotted the woody centre of the flax stalk, making it easier
to separate from the linen fibres. This horribly smelly process could take up to two weeks.

Look very carefully at the centre skyline in this view of Carrick-a-rede in the early twentieth century and you will see the tiny outlines of quarrymen working at the base of the dolorite sill of Knocksoghey, in a quarry known locally as 'Brockey'. The stone was cut into setts which were exported by sea to Scotland and used to pave Glasgow's streets.

The cone of the old Ballycastle glassworks, established by Hugh Boyd in 1755 to utilise local coal and other resources, such as kelp and sand. Although the glassworks closed after Boyd's death in 1766 the cone, which was sited on Glass Island, between the old dock (now the tennis courts) and the mouth of the Margy, was not demolished until 1877. This photograph was probably taken in 1875 when the photographer R.J. Welch visited the town as a boy of sixteen.

The beach from which Portballintrae ('port of the town of the strand') derived its name has now all but disappeared, carried away in huge quantities over the years for use in a variety of purposes. Here three carters have been caught in the act.

R.J. Maxwell's quarry at Coleraine, photographed in 1937. The quarry offices are dwarfed by the cutting-edge technology of the very latest in stone-crushing and screening machinery. Only the horse-drawn stone cart under the delivery shed serves as a reminder of times past.

Basalt was one of the Causeway Coast's major resources; in past times even the hexagonal pillars of the Giant's Causeway were heavily mined, for souvenirs as well as building rock. These drillers are cutting into the honeycomb of stone to obtain presentation pieces to send to Boston.

The smithy at the Columnar Basalt Company at Craigahulliar, outside Portrush, photographed in 1937. Basalt was an extremely durable stone, and was generally used in its rubble form for field walls, retaining walls and bridges. It was also dressed for use as building blocks, and crushed for road ballast.

The coal outcrops which run for 2 miles along the coast between Ballycastle and Fair Head have been mined horizontally since the 1600s. At its peak in the 1750s, over one hundred miners were employed to produce between 5,000 and 8,000 tons of coal per year. The view above is of the Gobb Colliery, one of a dozen known to have operated over the years.

Miners leaving the White Mine, the last working colliery in Ballycastle, which was re-opened during the Second World War to produce coal for local domestic use, and continued to be worked part-time until the mid-1950s.

The generating station on the Salmon Leap on the River Bush, a short distance outside Bushmills, produced power for the Giant's Causeway tramway. It opened in 1883 as the first hydro-electric station in the world to drive trams, and originally used two American Allcott turbines to drive a Siemens machine to generate current at 450 volts. It ceased operating in 1949, when the tramway closed.

CHAPTER EIGHT

TOWNSCAPE &
STREET SCENES

The clock says ten past twelve on a sunny day in the early 1900s, but there are few clues in this postcard view as to why such a crowd of neatly dressed men should gather at Coleraine Town Hall. Hiring fairs were held there, but the style of dress and the horse carriage on the left suggest a more formal occasion . . . perhaps a funeral?

The focal point of Coleraine is its magnificent town hall, built in 1859 to a design by Thomas Turner and shown here after W.J. Given's sensitive alterations in 1902 moved the entrance from the west to the east side. The irregularity in height of the buildings in the surrounding Diamond has been a feature of the town centre since the beginning of the nineteenth century.

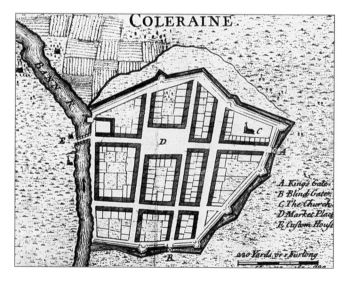

This contemporary survey shows how Coleraine was laid out by the London Livery Companies, who had been granted it and the surrounding district by James I in 1613, and were charged to 'build a town, to people it, to enclose it with a wall and to establish a market'. None of the original fabric of the town survives today, save its broad street plan and well-laid-out appearance.

Church Street in the early 1930s, looking towards the town hall, where a Catherwood's bus is stopped beside the war memorial. By 1928 Mr Catherwood, a native of Toome, was running bus services between all the major towns in Counties Antrim and Londonderry; also in the photograph are a bull-nosed Morris Cowley from County Armagh, on the left, and a County Derry-registered Austin on the right.

Continuity over thirty years is clearly expressed in this view of Church Street in the early 1960s. The town hall continues to dominate the scene; the Catherwood transport firm is still represented; the attraction of Coleraine for visitors is still revealed in car number plates, this time in regard to the County Tyrone-registered Anglia; and even the town hall clock tells the same time!

Taken from the top of the town hall, this panoramic view of Bridge Street and beyond in the 1880s shows the westward spread of Coleraine over the Bann and up past the courthouse, just below the horizon in the far distance. Note the paved pedestrian crossings at the lower far right and left of the photograph, and the glass roof and annexed darkroom of a photographer's studio at the top of the tall building on the upper right.

The opposing perspective to the previous image is truly a picture of contrasts with the thatched houses on the right of Captain Street Lower looking across to the stately new commercial and civic premises on the left. The pump spilling water into a broken trough is a reminder of the unhealthiness and inconvenience of life before water was piped to the home.

Looking north towards the mouth of the Bann, this aerial view of Coleraine in the 1960s pinpoints the main commercial role of the town: a bridge town for road and rail traffic and a natural market centre for its farming hinterland.

This lovely view of the River Bann's treacherous approach, with the hills of Donegal in the background, shows the Crannagh, home to Coleraine's ancient 'town' salmon fishery. Still worked, but considerably less productive than when this photograph was taken, the survival of this traditional enterprise and its setting highlights the success with which Coleraine's essentially rural nature has been preserved.

This up river view of the Bann snaking into Coleraine between the wooded slopes of Mountsandel on the far left and Somerset on the far right shows the landing stage of the Bann Rowing Club and, behind it, the old brick boathouse which was replaced in 1900 by the half-timbered structure shown on p. 66. The tall chimney belongs to Lawrence's Mill; to the right the gate-lodge entrance to Bannfield House, once the home of Samuel Lawrence, can be seen at the end of Hanover Place.

Coleraine Academical Institution opened in 1860 on a site donated by the London Clothworkers' Company. Its boarding tradition (which first cost 40 guineas per annum) has only recently ended. This photograph shows the school after the Old Boy's Wing, seen here on the left of the original building, was added in 1895. Extensive further additions in the last thirty years betoken the academic and sporting achievements of Coleraine Inst. (Reader, beware of any other school styling itself 'Inst.')

Phase One of the New University of Ulster, Northern Ireland's second university, opened with some 400 students in 1968 at Cromore, just outside Coleraine. Renamed the University of Ulster after the merger in 1984, it now has 19,500 students in four campuses – Coleraine, Magee, Jordanstown and York Street, Belfast.

Fison's dairy products, cheese and baby formula factory on Millburn Road, Coleraine, pictured in the late 1950s, with the railway bridge across the River Bann as an impressive backdrop. The rugby goalposts just above the river on the left mark the playing fields of Coleraine Inst.

The gasworks at Hanover Place supplied Coleraine with gas from the 1840s until its closure in the late 1980s. Its proximity to the harbour facilitated the necessary supply of coal from which the gas was made. The coke which was left over from the process was a popular form of cheaper home heating.

Coleraine Technical School was opened in November 1905 by Sir Horace Plunkett for the Department of Agricultural and Technical Instruction in Dublin. When it moved to new premises in Union Street, the original Lodge Road building became the police station – the 'barracks'!

Rodgers's Coleraine Shirt and Collar Manufactory provided female employment at its Beresford Road premises from the early 1900s until it closed in the late 1950s.

The sea-walk gracefully following the contours of the bay remains Portstewart's most enduring attraction, a constant source of bracing walks and pleasant drives for visitors and locals alike. This early view of the resort was taken before its famous stone promenade was built or its harbour redeveloped.

An early view of the Hill and Harryville in Portstewart, taken from the seaward end of Victoria Terrace. The tennis courts were later to be replaced by Atlantic Circle. The apparently abandoned camera case in the centre foreground suggests that the photographer has been forced to step as far back as he could to gain sufficient width for his shot. This somewhat unprepossessing image was later reproduced as a 'John Valentine' postcard.

Thackeray approved of these 'smart houses which face the beach westward' when he visited Portstewart in the 1840s. Sixty years later, when these smartly dressed promenaders took the air on a sunny afternoon, the resort was largely unchanged. Sweets and minerals were sold from the white hut on the left.

The group of people waiting for the Portstewart tram, which stopped here on its way from the depot to the railway station at Cromore, doubtless included holidaymakers, many of whom would have stayed in the lodging and guest-houses behind them in Atlantic Circle.

Burnside was founded by fishermen farmers from Dunboe, and was originally not only a village in its own right but also one of much greater importance than Portstewart, having an inn and other accommodation for visitors to the seaside. The jaunting car on the right is travelling up Larkhill, which was then part of the old Coleraine Road. Have the people walking behind got off to save the horse?

This view of Portstewart's Strand Road in the 1920s was taken from the lounge of the Strand Hotel, with its panoramic sea vistas, and shows new villas and bungalows strung out along what had previously been a sparsely developed coastline.

This view of Portrush from the impressive east strand illustrates the extent to which the town juts out to sea. This is possibly the most exposed position on a coastline well known for constant buffeting from wind and tide.

Here we see Portrush from the end of Bath Terrace to the broad sweep of the east strand, with a couple taking an evening stroll down the hill to the children's bathing place and, perhaps, the promise of refreshment in the Arcadia Café.

Main Street, Portrush, pictured on a sunny day before the First World War. The only wheeled transport is a horse cart. The shops in view include, on the left, MacAulay's chemist and, beside it, Portrush House, famous for Irish linens. On the right can be seen the Orchard Café and Billiard Hall, Black's Trocadero Lounge and, below that, the conical tower of the Northern Bank, designed by Vincent Craig.

Main Street, Portrush, looking south from the Northern Bank, with a family striking a charming pose for the photographer. Again, the lack of wheeled traffic is striking.

This view shows the lower end of Main Street and includes some of Portrush's best-known landmarks. At the extreme right can be seen the bow windows of the Northern Counties Hotel; protruding in the centre is the portico of the White House, the town's most prestigious shop, opened in 1891 by Henry Hamilton, who also owned the White House and the Windsor Hotels. On the left stands Caskey's drapery and fancy goods shop, with its wooden canopy over the breadth of the footpath.

The poles carrying the overhead lines supplying power to the Causeway tram are gaily decked in this photograph of Causeway Street in the 1920s. The mixture of housing styles is quite striking, but this is one of Portrush's oldest thoroughfares. The original name of the street lives on in the Springhill Bar, which is the large building in the background on the right, its gable wall painted with an advertisement for Bushmills whiskey.

Thatched houses huddle across the road in the tiny village of Dunseverick. Note the roofs of roped thatch, and the way the building at the end has been built at right angles to the others to provide shelter. A Scotch cart leans against the house on the left, while a jaunting car is parked on the right.

Portballintrae in the 1890s, looking down towards the fishermen's cottages at the bottom of the hill in a view that has changed remarkably little over the years. Beloved as a peaceful retreat by generations of holidaymakers, Portballintrae has the dubious distinction of being the only place in Ireland to be shelled during the First World War when a German U-boat opened fire on the coaster *Wheatear* as she sailed from Coleraine.

The road snakes down to Ballintoy village before turning and dropping like a stone to the harbour in the distance. The linear development of local settlement is well illustrated in this stunning view, which still hints at ancient patterns of land use represented by grazing on the inland side of the road and strip-farming of arable land on the seaward.

The so-called 'artist's house' being built at Ballintoy harbour. Newton Penpraze was a successful, if eccentric, artist who fell in love with the rugged seascape at Ballintoy because it reminded him of his native Cornwall. When completed, his house was full of idiosyncratic – though nearly always practical – features, one of which was a stairway in the cliff linking the house directly with a beautiful but otherwise inaccessible cove below.

Bushmills was accused in the late nineteenth century of comprising one main street 974 yards in length, but this contemporary view shows the inland town sprawled over the countryside from the market tower on the extreme right to the chimney of the 'Old Bushmills' distillery on the extreme left.

Traditionally, whiskey has been made in Bushmills since 1608, though the present distillery itself dates from 1784. Most of the whitewashed buildings shown here were built after a devastating fire in 1855. The pagoda-like malt-house roofs are distinctive. The present distillery can produce one million gallons of the 'craythur' annually.

This distinctive, if slightly dumpy, clock tower, an imitation Irish round tower, was erected in Bushmills by the local landlord, Sir Francis McNaughten, in 1874. It stands guard at the entrance to Market Square. By the end of the nineteenth century two weekly agricultural markets were held here, with a fair on the 15th of each month. It was a small but busy and prosperous little town, with three mills, two bicycle works, a spade mill, a regular tourist trade and a rich farming hinterland.

This postcard of Bushmills at the beginning of the twentieth century was sent to a friend in Dublin by 'Maureen' in 1938 with the observation 'The photo is old. Bushmills hasn't changed a bit.'

The full extent of Ballycastle's imposing geographical position, perched high on the coast in the most north-easterly part of Ireland, is revealed in this aerial view of the harbour area. The ruins of Duneanie Castle, from which the town derived its name, stood at the top of the headland north of the jetty, in a prime defensive position.

This view of Ballycastle looks down Quay Hill and over the harbour to the ruins of Bonamargy Abbey in the centre distance. The building on the extreme left is the forge where the horses employed at the jetty were shod; the stone house to its right is the coastguard station.

The best view of Ballycastle, so it has been said, was from the Fair Hill, where almost a century ago the photographer stood to take this charming picture. The church of St Mary and St Brigid, with the parochial house beside, sits proudly on the brow of the hill; Fairhill Street, to the right, runs past the Schoolhouse, down to the Diamond, marked by the three-storeyed white building below the chapel.

A fine view of the Diamond with Hugh Boyd's Holy Trinity Church framed by a street scene only slightly marred by the obtrusive entrance to the bakery on the left. The monument in front of the church was erected by public subscription to Dr George O'Connor, medical superintendent at Ballycastle Workhouse (1844–97), and cut and built by two local masons, Charles Darragh and Andrew Verdon. It cost £352.

North Street, Ballycastle, looking towards Market Corner, with the town's last thatched house on the right. The house, with its new slate roof, still stands.

Ardihannon post office opened in 1896, presumably in part to serve the growing army of visitors to the Giant's Causeway, and was one of three independent sub-post offices in the immediate vicinity. The Causeway Memorial School, which adjoins it to the left, was built in 1914/15 to a design by Clough Williams Ellis. Dedicated to Lord McNaughton of Runkerry, its entrance was flanked by two engravings by the Holywood artist Rosamund Praeger, famous for her depictions of children.

The blacksmith standing outside the forge at Dunluce is having his likeness captured by camera and by pen in this early photograph of an highly unusual building. One small window to the left of the door admits the only light he has to work by, save the glow of the fire.

A row of fishermen's cottages at the Aird, close to the Giant's Causeway, with some tourists from Pittsburgh, USA, talking to the woman in the goffered linen cap in the centre. According to the photographer, the big black pot beside them was used to boil potatoes for the pigs.

R.J. Welch visited Rathlin in 1889, and took this photograph of 'Paddy the Cliff Climber', shown here with his fowling rope, with Dr Lloyd Praeger, on the left with a stick, and Robert Patterson with his geological hammer. The house, with its splashes of whitewash only around the windows, is typical of older island homes. Note the barrel serving as a chimney.

CHAPTER NINE

STOP A-WHILE

The smiling hostess of Dunluce House, one of the oldest surviving private dwellings on the Causeway Coast, with a sign made out of a carpet-beater. The inscription above the door reads 'This bwildit [built] by M.H and B.T. 1623', dating the house to a time when Dunluce Castle was occupied and the adjacent settlement was a town of considerable stature.

Giant's Well, *c.* 1890. From the eighteenth century local men and women acted as guides and hosts to tourists at the Giant's Causeway. While their zeal in selling their services was often criticised by visitors, this lady selling refreshments seems a model of decorum. Her white pleated bonnet is in a style traditional to fishing communities throughout Ireland and Britain, reinforcing the notion that these communities often had more in common with each other than with the land-locked regions which surrounded them.

Giant's Well, *c.* 1935. The scenery is the same (although the hard stones have been softened by planks of wood) and so is the action in this later view of visitors being offered the waters at the Giant's Causeway.

'The Grand Hotel', photographed on a Naturalists' Field Club visit to Rathlin Island in 1936, was owned by the McCuaigs, and may have been christened such by its visitors – who actually stayed in a chalet at the rear – because it overlooked the harbour and Mount Grand.

In 1746 Rathlin Island was sold to the Gage family, who started to build the Manor House in 1763. The house was based on a row of weaver's cottages, which may explain its long, low outline. This photograph was taken in about 1895, and shows visitors being ferried from the old coastguard pier by local boatmen, among them Michael Jack Anderson, Joseph McCurdy and John Black.

Few youth hostels enjoyed such a sumptuous view, or such an illustrious history, as that at Whitepark Bay. The building previously housed a school for the sons of local gentry which opened in the mid-eighteenth century and reputedly provided the early education for such notables as Edward McNaughten, Lord of the Treasury, Sir Francis McNaughten, chief justice of Calcutta, and the Hon. Robert Stewart, later Lord Castlereagh.

Such was the demand for accommodation from the influx of summer visitors to the triangle area of Portrush and Portstewart in the early 1960s that 'shanty towns', as they were condemned in the press, began to spring up on unlicensed caravan sites on coastal ground between the towns. Note the two railway carriages serving as chalets on the right of the central group.

Picnic tables in lay-bys became a feature of tourist provision on the Causeway Coast from the 1960s. Here a family from the Dublin area enjoys a surprisingly elaborate open-air meal, as the assortment of crockery, pots and pans indicates.

Situated just outside Portrush, Juniper Hill Caravan Holiday Camp, as it was originally styled, was established on 17 acres of land provided by Londonderry County Council in 1950 'as a first step in the projected clearance of [the] unsightly developments' pictured opposite. The site could accommodate 300 caravans, and was provided with first-class sanitary and toilet facilities, including hot water showers, as well as the children's playground shown here on the right.

Built at a cost of £2,000 in 1844, the year Coleraine's old wooden bridge was replaced, the Clothworker's Hotel was constructed by John Lynn, who was also the designer of the town's new stone bridge. Until the railway bridge was built across the river in 1860, the hotel marked the end of the line for trains from and to Londonderry.

One of Ballycastle's oldest surviving hostelries, the Antrim Arms was built in 1754 and extensively altered in 1853 when water closets were added to its existing amenities. The first horse of the pair harnessed to the jaunting car in this 1890s photograph is a trace horse, whose additional pulling power helped haul passengers up Ballycastle's steep hills.

The River Bush was famous for salmon, and anglers came to Bushmills from all over the British Isles to try its sport. The Bushmills Hotel, with its flight of stone steps leading to the riverside, catered directly for their trade.

The Carrick-a-Rede Hotel in Ballintoy, one of the town's main buildings, was built by Edmund McCambridge, owner of the Boyd Arms in Ballycastle. Directly opposite was the town's other hotel, the Fullerton Arms, named after Dr Alexander Fullerton of Jamaica who had purchased Ballintoy Castle from the Stewarts in the mid-eighteenth century. Both hotels catered primarily for tourists and day-trippers.

Kane's Royal Hotel, photographed after renovations for the 1890 season furnished it with two large coffee rooms, ladies' drawing rooms and bathrooms with hot and cold water. The original hotel was a farmhouse which had been converted by Mary Jane Campbell, owner of the Antrim Arms in Bushmills, after she married Francis Kane of Ardihannon in 1863; when the Prince of Wales, later Edward VII, visited the Causeway she took him in for tea and asked his permission to call her establishment 'Royal'. Keen rivalry – and not a little ill will – existed between this hotel and Mr Traill's Causeway Hotel, which it overlooked, and which the Kanes eventually bought in 1910.

The Portrush Golf and Hydropathic Hotel opened on this commanding position overlooking the West Strand in 1893. Its proximity to the recently opened Portrush golf links boosted its attractiveness to holidaymakers, while the spa treatments it also promised were a popular Victorian seaside amenity.

Part of a series of publicity photographs taken at the end of July 1934, this somewhat clinical view of the refurbished Portrush Hotel (much better known as Fawcett's Hotel) surrounded by deserted streets belies the fact that the holiday season was at its height in the town. Perhaps it was very early in the morning.

The façade of the plain-looking Londonderry Hotel in Main Street, c. 1895. It typified the moderately priced family accommodation Portrush offered when its popularity as a holiday resort soared towards the end of the nineteenth century.

The glamour and gaiety of a holiday in Portrush is emphasised in this view of the brightly decorated Seabank Hotel on Bath Street in May 1933. The hotel, with its uninterrupted sea views, was built as a private house in 1890; in 1937 it boasted central heating, an electric lift, a ballroom and an orchestra. In 1968 it became a hall of residence for students at the New University of Ulster in Coleraine, before being converted into a private nursing home.

Cloughorr House, looking somewhat dishevelled here, was turned into a hotel by its owner, Mrs J. Rankin, who also ran a dairy and a milk-run. Its prosperity was assured when the Royal Portrush Golf Club moved to new premises on the opposite side of the Bushmills Road and the hotel, now renamed the Golf Links, was able to offer accommodation to players. It is undoubtedly best known as Kelly's Disco, one of Northern Ireland's must-be places for generations of young (and young-at-heart) clubbers.

The Ladies' Bathing Place, as it was called when this photograph was taken in 1900, was, in many respects, the heart of Portrush as a seaside resort. The grassy sloping bank overlooking it was the site of the town's first 'respectable' lodging house, built by the Misses Ryan in 1822. The wooden hut beside the stone building advertising Cantrell & Cochrane's was the forerunner of the town's famous Arcadia Café, with its balcony and breathtaking views.

The Arcadia, pictured here days before it was knocked down in the early 1990s, became one of the most popular entertainment venues on the Causeway Coast, particularly in the heyday of the dance-band era of the 1950s and 1960s. A true 'ballroom-of-romance', it spent its last few years as a leisure centre and amusement hall, before being condemned and demolished.

Built in 1837 as the Antrim Arms Hotel, the Northern Counties Hotel in Portrush was taken over and enlarged by the directors of the Northern Counties railway company when the trains reached the town in 1855. This photograph was taken not long after the hotel was reconstructed in 1892 to designs by John Lanyon. With its commanding position, lavish interiors, glittering clientele and air of comprehensive luxury, the Northern Counties gained a reputation as 'the heart of Portrush'. The gaping hole left in the townscape when it was completely destroyed by fire in 1990 has yet to be filled.

The Marine Hotel was built in 1892 and was Ballycastle's largest and most modern hotel. Situated on the corner of Quay Road and North Road, it offered easy access to all the attractions that the resort offered. It aimed itself especially at the British coaching trade and in the 1930s it was the headquarters of the Belfast concern of 'Upton's Reliable Irish Tours'; this market collapsed with the start of the 'Troubles' and the Marine closed in 1972 when all its bookings were cancelled. It was later destroyed in one of Ballycastle's few terrorist bomb attacks.

CHAPTER TEN

WISH YOU WERE HERE

*There must be holiday snaps of children perched on donkeys on the broad, sandy beaches of
Portrush in family albums throughout the country and beyond.*

Designed by Berkeley D. Wise in 1894 when the rear of the hotel was extended, the glorious ballroom in the Northern Counties Hotel, with its sprung dance floor and gilded surroundings, saw generations of locals and visitors swing to the music of guest and resident bands.

The Arcadia in Portrush, pictured here during an energetic dance night in the 1950s, was consistently one of the most popular 'boy-meets-girl' spots on the Causeway Coast, when holiday romance might blossom to the sounds of skiffle.

The Skating Rink and Pleasure Grounds in Portrush's Station Square were well patronised, as this early postcard view suggests, but were never a financial success. Barry's Amusements now occupies their site. The Station 'Café' on the left, used for a host of recreational, educational and sporting activities, was demolished in the 1970s.

Originally the Majestic Cinema and Snack Bar, Portrush's Playhouse Cinema, situated on Main Street beside the White House, was completely refurbished in the early 1970s. From the state of the weather in this photograph, it could not open a day too soon.

The tinkling of the bell on the children's railway must be for many people one of the sounds most redolent of a summer visit to Portrush. It was located just outside both the railway station and Barry's Amusements, to which all youngsters hoped one day to graduate or remain for ever a train driver.

The safe and sheltered children's bathing place in Portrush, even in Victorian times, as this 1880s view shows, was an enduring attraction where children could experience for the first time the thrill of waves lapping at their feet.

Barry's Amusement World was strategically located between Portrush railway station and the west strand. From its beginnings as a small funfair in the 1920s this grew into one of the biggest, scariest and best-loved fairground attractions in Ireland, with its tempting range of state-of-the-art rides and games.

A teeming Portrush west strand on a glorious summer day, with the helter-skelter and big wheel of Barry's towering in the background beside the station. The two dark-suited and behatted ladies in the centre of the view seem to be taking no chances with the weather!

Tennis was one of the many diversions listed in a 1950 promotional guide to Portstewart, where this view of the resort's public courts first appeared.

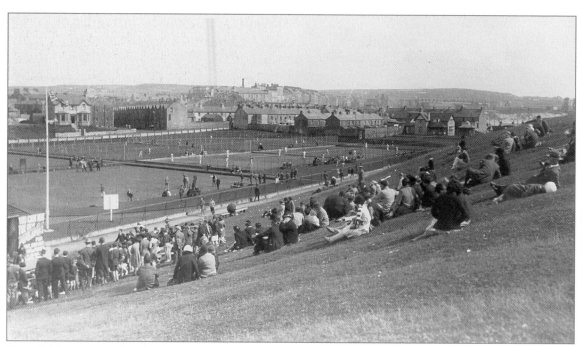

Part of the recreational grounds constructed at the foot of Ramore Head in Portrush after the First World War. The bowling greens were 'laid with Cumberland turf – the best in the world for bowls'. Tennis courts and putting greens were also provided.

The first ladies' clubhouse at Portrush was a wood and tin hut vacated by gentlemen golfers in 1892. In 1928 it was replaced by a handsome brick building on the Bushmill Road, pictured here shortly after it opened.

The County Golf Club was formed in Portrush in 1898 and became the Royal Portrush in 1895 with the patronage of Edward, Prince of Wales. In 1948 the links course was radically remodelled, and the club's headquarters transferred to the former Holywood Hotel on the Bushmills Road. The original building can be seen to the left of the 1960s extension highlighted in this view.

The 'North-West 200' was first raced in 1929 and is now one of the biggest and certainly the fastest motorcycle road races in the British Isles. Recognised as Ireland's most-watched sporting event, the circuit rings Portstewart, Coleraine and Portrush and contains many hotly contested prime vantage points, such as this screeching bend at Henry's Corner to Portstewart promenade.

Another screeching bend, this time high above the beach at Portrush, as four girls enjoy the excitement of a ride on the big dipper at Barry's.

Held during the last week of August, Ballycastle's Lammas Fair survives as one of the most eagerly awaited gatherings marking the ancient Irish festival of Lughansa, the beginning of harvest. Originally lasting for six days, it became a two-day affair after the First World War, the first for business and the second for pleasure. The three items most popularly associated with the fair – courting, an edible, dried seaweed called dulse and yellow man, a type of very sweet and very chewy toffee candy – were immortalised in the chorus of John Henry McAuley's famous ballad 'The Ould Lammas Fair'.

At the Ould Lammas Fair in Ballycastle long ago
I met a little colleen who set my heart aglow
She was smiling at her daddy buying lambs from Paddy Roe,
At the Ould Lammas Fair in Ballycastle O!
I seen her home that night when the moon was shining bright
From the Ould Lammas Fair at Ballycastle O.

Chorus

At the Ould Lammas Fair, boys, were you ever there,
At the Ould Lammas Fair in Ballycastle O?
Did you treat your Mary Ann to dulse and yellow man
At the Ould Lammas Fair in Ballycastle, O?

In Flanders fields afar, while resting from the war,
We drank Bon Sante to the Flemish lasses, O!
But the scene that haunts my memory is kissing Mary Ann,
Her pouting lips all sticky from eating yellow man,
As we crossed the silver Margy and strolled along the strand,
From the Ould Lammas Fair at Ballycastle, O.

Chorus

There's a nate little cabin on the slopes of ould Knocklayde
It's lit by love and sunshine where the heather honey's made,
By the bees ever humming and our childhers' joyous call,
Resounds across the valley when the shadows fall;
I take my fiddle down and my Mary smiling there,
Brings back the happy mem'ry of the Lammas Fair.

The Giant's Causeway was first described to the scientific world in 1693 and became one of the main geological sites to confirm the volcanic origin of basalt. It was acquired by the National Trust in 1961, and was declared a World Heritage Site by UNESCO in 1987. Its stark grandeur is well captured in this aerial view, which shows the three main amphitheatres curving from the little schoolhouse perched on top of the cliffs on the extreme right to the headland of Port na Spania just out of picture on the extreme left.

Acclaimed as an open textbook for the study of geology because of the number, range and clarity of the separate features it displays, the columnar nature of the Giant's Causeway and the stratifications of the surrounding cliffs are well illustrated in this 1909 view of the horizontal formations. The house in the picture was removed by the National Trust in an attempt to restore the natural appearance of the site.

These two images of women seated at the Wishing Chair at the Giant's Causeway were taken within a few years of each other at the beginning of the twentieth century, and both were presented in postcard format. The one to the right is the work of the Portrush commercial photographer Lee, who provided summer visitors to this popular attraction with pictorial reminders of their stay. The one below was published as one of a famous series of 'Irish Views' by the Belfast photographer R.J. Welch, who enlisted as his models the notorious Causeway guides who quickly realised the commercial potential of the view on their doorstep, and cannily exploited a staged Irish quaintness for the delectation of tourists.

ACKNOWLEDGEMENTS

The authors would like to thank the following people for their invaluable help and support in producing this book. While all our colleagues in the National Museums and Galleries of Northern Ireland gave unstintingly of their advice and support, we are especially grateful to Robert Heslip, Tom Wylie, Pauline Dickson and Jane Leonard of the Department of History; Richard Warner, Cormac Bourke, Sinead McCartan, Winifred Glover and Deirdre Crone of the Department of Archaeology and Ethnography; Catherine McCullough and Greer Ramsey of Armagh County Museum; and Peter Crowther and Ken James of the Department of Geology for their patient assistance and good humour in answering our queries on such a wide range of subjects. We would also like to extend a special thank-you to our National Museums and Galleries of Northern Ireland colleagues at the Ulster Folk and Transport Museum for their help, particularly Mark Kennedy, who gave his expert knowledge of road, rail and air transport so freely. The technical skills and remarkable tolerance of Bill Porter, Michael McKeown and Bryan Rutledge of the Ulster Museum's Photographic Department, and of Ken Anderson, George Wright and Alan McCartney, their counterparts at the Ulster Folk and Transport Museum, who supplied the bulk of the prints used in this book to such quality, often at ridiculously short notice, are also gratefully acknowledged. We are also extremely grateful to Walter McAulay and the staff of the Editorial Library of the *Belfast Telegraph* for their help in locating and printing the archive images reproduced in this volume. Thanks are also due to Sandra Neill and Patricia McLean of the Ulster Museum's Marketing Department for their close attention to issues of copyright and contract. We would also like to thank Alex Morrison, David Laing, Mr A. Logan, Peter Roebuck, Bill Crawford, George Dunlop, and Eileen and Daniel Fisher for the information they so kindly provided.

We also relied heavily on printed sources for information, and would like to acknowledge our particular debt in this respect to the published work of Robert Anderson, Jonathan Bell, Wallace Clark, Cahal Dallat, W.D. Girvan, Fred Hamond, Myrtle Hill, Michael McCaughan, W.A. McCutcheon, Tom McDonald, Bill Maguire, Grenfell Morton, J.E. Mullin and T.H. Mullin, Brian Turner and Ian Wilson. Special thanks are also due to Helen Perry of the Causeway Museum Service, for the last-minute loan of material from the Sammy Walker collection of photographs.

Responsibility for error or omission rests, of course, with the authors, who would be pleased to receive any further information on the photographs published. Readers may also like to know that the photographic collections of the National Museums and Galleries of Northern Ireland may be consulted by appointment with either the History Department of the Ulster Museum or the Library at the Ulster Folk and Transport Museum, and that reproduction prints of most of the images contained therein can be obtained.